The Rangeley Lakes: Twenty Photo Essays on Love of Land
Text and photographs ©2012 George Adams
ISBN 978-1-938883-00-2

Email: gadams28@gmail.com

Cover: Mooselookmeguntic Lake, June 2012

All rights reserved. No part of this book may be reproduced in any form or by any electronic or mechanical means, including information storage and retrieval systems, without permission in writing from the author, except by a reviewer, who may quote brief passages in review.

Designed and Produced by
Maine Authors Publishing
558 Main Street, Rockland, Maine 04841
www.maineauthorspublishing.com

The Rangeley Lakes

Twenty Photo Essays on Love of Land

George Adams

Rangeley, 2012

To John and Jean,
old friends
so good to see
again,
George

Dedication

May this book stand in support of the legacy the
Rangeley Lakes Heritage Trust provides for everyone,
the preservation and protection
of the land and its wilderness,
forever.

And also to
Ruth,
who gave me
the out-of-doors.

Contents

Introduction • 1
All Beautiful the March of Days • 2
Moon Reflections • 4
More than Chasing Sunsets • 6
Iris in the Wild • 8
Snow Everywhere • 10
A Child's World • 12
Leaves Falling • 14
Canoeing into New Land • 16
We Live in a Land I • 18
We Live in a Land II • 20
A Loon Nesting Triumph • 22
Adult Loons Gathering • 24
Loon Wing Act • 26
The Seasons Follow • 28
Snowshoe Pathways • 30
Wildlife Encounter at Hunter Cove • 32
Winter Clings Its Best • 34
Catching a Blue Heron in Flight • 36
An Overlook of Beauty • 38
Mooselookmeguntic Lake • 40
Epilogue • 43

Introduction

Each of us has a special place, one that heals the spirit and quiets the mind. My own arose from an invite at age twelve to an old and quaint homestead in southern New Hampshire, through the generosity of a lady admirer who took a shine to my situation. And so was born a liking for the country and the out-of-doors, one that you will see lasted a lifetime. I later wrote of this as My Special Place.

Over time the sentiments remained, enabling Maine places to dominate my feelings, in preserving that which I found soft and sacred. I began recording my sentiments via camera of my Maine Special Place.

The serenity of a snowed-in country home nestled among trees. A running stream and clinging snow. A blue heron in tilted flight. The low sun and its glorious assortments.

But the camera was barely sufficient, as my instinct for beauty brought forth its own prose, to compliment and enhance what my mind also conceived, and the paring more than doubled the appeal.

With no intent to assemble for the future, I came to realize that I was giving birth to my own stand-alone photo essays, being tales of life in the make-believe, being unique tokens of charm and elegance in the mountains with their willing and ancient creatures.

In time I assembled twenty of these occurrences, each written on a flair of unexaggerated excitement, now to became a unique storybook tale of where peace-loving folks reside.

Such tales now follow, to bring you fulfillment, that someone in earnest could foresee.

All Beautiful the March of Days

All beautiful the march of days, as seasons come and go;
The Hand that shaped the rose hath wrought the crystal of the snow;
Hath sent the hoary frost of Heav'n, the flowing waters sealed,
And laid a silent loveliness on hill and wood and field.

O'er white expanses sparkling pure the radiant morns unfold;
The solemn splendor of the night burn brighter than the cold;
Life mounts in every throbbing vein, love deepens round the hearth,
And clearer sounds the angel hymn, "Good will to men on earth."

O Thou from Whose unfathomed law the year in beauty flows,
Thyself the vision passing by in Crystal and in rose,
Day unto day doth utter speech, and night to night proclaim,
In ever changing words of light, the wonder of Thy Name.

—Frances W. Wile

(This essay only is not original with the author.)

Written as a hymn extolling the beauty of winter in 1910 at the request of her pastor, and appears in the Rangeley Congregational Church New Century Hymnal (NCH #434)

Moon Reflections

Taken in late summer, this one reflection in particular became a unique scene of Rangeley Lake, for, despite many attempts, it has never been possible to obtain again its many features with a clear and perfect sky and at full moon time that sets coincident with the rising sun. Attributes of value include numerous features of note. The ruffled water pleasantly disturbs the bright beam on its way to the shore; its location beside and not through the island and so full in length; the reflection timing with sunrise, which has only begun, and so the adjoining terrain is barely discernable; the mountainous background, signifying remoteness and northern climes; the foreground trees so properly aligned and adding to depth. Of course, the all-important sharpness to the reflection adds detail as it meanders across the surface.

At this far-off land and latitude, one finds many lake moods occurring throughout the years, offering a constant variety of change to those with patience and fortitude to remember over time. Mighty lake moods include observing in summer ominous down-lake storms of lightning streaks with calamitous thunder, a front of heavy winds and sheets of driving rain moving across lake, mixed up ice and its upheavals, springtime melting and its odd patterns, an abundance of setting sun effects. Clearly a different sunset glow occurs each night, sometimes enhanced with colors reflected from clouds above, and sometimes soft and endearing in shades of magnificence with feelings. This scene, labeled "Moon Reflections," was taken from the eastern hillside, with height enough to encompass distance to the far shore yet sufficiently narrow to define the island by which the reflection travels. Others times the setting occurs not so favorably with the island.

This picture, taken years ago, finally gained attention and so received these words. The enrichment and charisma emerged, giving it value in its beauty in the tale seen above, so all can witness and come to cherish our land and its cool moods of artistry and charm. (2011)

More than Chasing Sunsets

Sunset in November coincides with my daily visit to Rangeley's wellness center, wherein all spectacular lake beauty may be witnessed from lake-facing side of this wonderful establishment. During late afternoon is best for me, as I found myself unknowingly in early November chasing over three days sunsets that were irresistible. When the sun dips below the horizon the action begins, as the cloud's underside becomes a cataclysmic triumph. I learned to end my rehab work just when the best part was playing out, namely when the colors were most intense and the cloud placement and lake surface were most reflective and when the peripheral trees gave the whole a special bearing, all the while a hint of blue emerged during the cloud openings. Being two-thirds sky made little difference, for the lakeshore outline and its one prominent island spoke for themselves

A picture is my favorite. There is no better conveyance of joy than the innocence of an immense scene, one that encompasses depth, emotion, and a certain balance with nature. These are my life. They bring me along and give me faith as I do unto others. I can enable you to see goodness and an awareness of life in the world around us. Beauty and nature speak to all of us. (2009)

Iris in the Wild

Nature gives back, if you give it your best hand with simple acts. Easing amiably at her reins, she will respond in like manner. The deed related here occurred just as told, and a voice from nature spoke back in warmth.

It was lunchtime of our kayak trip. We wanted a soft earth spot, and when we found it, we were a happy group. It was under trees and on spongy moss with a comforting view of the pond we traveled. After our laughter and listening to idle talk, we prepared to resume our water travels in the soft breeze. Once seated and ready for the push out, I noticed a stem and flower within arm's reach, all flat and desperate from our clumsy entrance. The stem was broken, but the petals were intact, as if speaking out in earnest.

Our group of nine boats and twelve people were on the Cupsuptic River near Moocher's camp in late June. It was remote and not near man-made effects. The rescue consisted of placing the stem in a bottle of river water, while realizing this wild beauty as exquisite in nature's repertoire, and almost missed. Once home its charms became forever, as its lavender shade and white lines reminded of who we are and why we go to these precious places and return enriched in heart. A near miss that returned a jewel. (2010)

Snow Everywhere

Did you know you can find snow everywhere,
Including under and over
all nature's beauty?
Did you know you can find snow in the winter,
Under trees and amongst small and large rocks
Of the land?
Did you know you can find snow wherever you are,
and especially
In locations where beauty is its best,
Like along a small stream of the roadside
In the lateness of the hour
when melting occurs?
Here the secrets of water run slowly away,
And the mounds of winter
heap between the pools of cool glory,
And especially after a recent falling of flakes.
Here all branches and things are draped
In the charm of this wholesome wonder,
Giving us its reflections
of goodness to carry
in our lives for all our days
under and around and
everywhere.

A Child's World

A sunset confronts us.
What to do?
Use an imagination
To the joy of you.

Let it all become a child's playroom
In which to learn and grow.
The lower streaking clouds just above the horizon become
Trolley cars in the sky, taking puppy dogs hither to
Home and love.
The canopy above is not afire,
But a woven fabric of gold
Made by mothers of kangaroos and rabbits.
To enjoin all the oddities underneath.
Bring forth a large pond, seen perhaps as a puddle,
For giant great whales to share and play,
And devour white frogs and worms.
Give the horizon some
Poking ears on the right,
Little men to oversee the new and
Comfortable world created from
An imagination run wild in joyful high jinx
Among zoo-like characters and more.

Leaves Falling

Leaves falling everywhere,
On the ground, in the air,
Swirling sideways and upside down,
Leaves seesawing to the ground.

I found a leaf and took it home.
It was some joy I wished to own.
Remember the beauty seen all around.
Find a leaf and take it home.

Canoeing into New Land
Aziscohos Lake

A new land became a dreamland, being desolate with deep blue sky and soft sandy shores, holding back towering pines amongst smaller ones in bright color, haunting as it was in its unfamiliar shorelines and with abruptly deep water. These were the forbidden places far from civilization and motion. Few adventures occur here; only the trudging moose and bear travel these hills in the cold in search of dominance. Only game hunters and those in love of the land venture into these waterways. My partner, a part-time guide in real life, and I came for reassurance, to get away and return renewed.

The mid-October day was warm and clear as we first wove into the lee of a connecting cove before emerging upon the mighty river Aziscohos and the hard push against wind to an ideal sandy beach, to be our northern most respite in the low sun of late afternoon. Once arrived and with our canoe secure, we were content in our feelings and place of peace. A small hassock of coarse grass held the thermos of warm tea as our feet dug in and our minds opened up to sharing.

It came that my partner loved these waters like no other, possessed as he was with future dreams and a destiny of hope. He told of an old map he was once given as a boy, a scaling of the mountains and water bodies around us that is invaluable today. We shared together the story of Bosebuck, a working hunting camp that we passed on the western shore in our travel an hour earlier. Named Bosebuck Camps, it was all of a hundred years ago that a hunting dog name Bose was charged to drive a huge buck to an exhausted state and sufficiently barked until his party arrived to take the beast for its field value and nourishment, hence the dog and subsequently the camp became Bosebuck. The tale was most fitting as we gazed on the large earth masses to the west and north in a personal reflective mood of silence, both of us content and unashamed of our preferences and instinct for what we were amidst and revered.

As the sun lowered, we left our comfort and glided south, still on the mainstream, and were about to take a detour across Sunday Pond. Instantly, we flushed a species of over twenty ducks that made flight in a rapid whirl, veering in unison before disappearing into a yonder of all their own. In only an instant they were both present and gone, leaving only a mind picture behind.

As the sun touched the hills and its warmth receded, we departed a place of pastoral and simple grace. And so it was necessary to put to words soon thereafter a document to preserve a state of mind and the remote setting as it was, especially to accompany some carefully recorded scenes that tell all. If I never return, others can enjoy in their own manner, and that gives me an added measure of pleasure in my deed to you and others. (2010)

We Live in a Land I

We live in a land of make-believe,
where one day turns into another of incredible charm,
where the sparkle of winter becomes the reassurance of spring,
and the brief emergence of warm months turns into colors of expiration.
Here the snows of heavy-laden spruces
cascade downward in the low midday sun.
At year's end we trudge through fields and frozen coves
with tree in hand just before dark.
We startle the great blue heron into flight,
or witness the graceful spiral of a golden eagle and then its
captive grasp.

With patience we sit and wait as the mother merganser
circles a vast shoreline with her dwindling brood,
and we listen for the owl's remote hoot,
or at midnight choose between the coyote's cry
and the loon's entertaining laugh.
Black flies, in the words of Thoreau,
are more formidable than wolves.
If not enough, there is scarlet lupine on roadsides,
and wild yellow iris aligning a favorite pond,
and each month the graceful reflection of a setting full moon
is timed with sunrise.

We Live in a Land II

We live in a land of make-believe,
Where a barred owl can look in your window,
And magnificent sunsets are as numerous
As nighttime stars,
Where moose rarely can be viewed with their
nursing young.
Where bobcats can be made accustomed to feed at your door.
Here loons are seen to dance on water for minutes at a time,
When mating is that time of year.

In a world of uncertainty and alarm,
Take time to observe the quiet land,
The steady water, the rolling hills, the still leaves and
The slowly winding lakeside shore.
Canoe to the further reaches on a lonely river,
And observe a flock of rare ducks be flushed and head south.
Take with you lunch and a friend and dig your feet into warm sand,
While enriched at night by the resounding ring of a loon's call
For a mate down lake.
Some of us find a view of heavenly falling snow or a
family of wild cormorants or a sudden moose or perhaps the
quiet peace of it all as you sit and
wait for nothing significant to happen.

A Loon Nesting Triumph
Beaver Mt. Lake

It was early afternoon with partial clouds and a still surf, both ideal conditions for searching out a nesting loon known to be secluded in the outlet marsh of a medium size lake near Rangeley. Little did my partner and I know she would depart the nest the next day, taking along two healthy and furry chicks, the result of some four weeks of incubation, sitting only inches above a water level that could rise and threaten.

We moved casually as the shoreline narrowed at the lake's outlet end, an ideal place for loon nesting away from open water with access to a quieter waterway. Cautiously peeping, we slowly proceeded and then there she was, patiently nestled among tall grass and on a prepared bed of softness, large and appealing. Immediately she was amply aware of our presence. This keepsake of beauty was visibly disturbed, displaying an open beak of anger and a sternness that was almost frightening. And yet her beauty was absolute and astounding. Most obvious was her panned-out body, a spreading of largeness that displayed a huge girth, mostly hidden from view when water bound.

She was positioned in offering to us her age-old markings, as if in defiance to predators of all types. Continuous white stripes flowed like water along her body while merging with a solid white underbody, a work of art tracing over millions of years with hardly any altered details. Clearly discernable was her necklace of white vertical stripes, all against the black body of a moonless night. The beauty converged with wing feathers, white spotted and of the same deep purity. So stunning she was in her adornments and their placement and glaring beauty. As we loitered there, she retained her nesting position, aware of a pending hatch while anxious of leaving home for the accustomed water life and greater safety. Tomorrow the scene did change, as a family of four becoming a new being, the young in time joining their counterparts in joyful play.

Loons are remembered in many ways, like the first time as a teenager becoming bewildered by the haunting howl in the middle of the night, or viewing the water dance of mate selection lasting for many minutes. I became a lover of loons at a young age, when I stood on a dock one morning in a thick fog looking outward. First coming into view were the proud parents marching along, and then the trailing week-old chicks, carefree and confident. Their assuring look all around was evident as they viewed the silent land as forever.

Two days later we returned, to find the foursome on the water and a part of the lake life not far from their nesting spot. In obvious happiness together, the little denizens were always within a few feet of their guardians, anxious to learn of life and enlarge their world. Staying surface bound, they took small nourishments from the parents while joining an ancient niche that faced few natural predators in returning year after year to a place established and satisfying. An enrichment it is to follow an age-old ritual of intimacy in the presence of great beauty. (2011)

Adult Loons Gathering
Rangeley Lake

The tremolos were unmistakable but the source was nowhere to be seen. Perhaps to the far left was a gathering of full-grown loons, slowly coming into view as my quiet kayak travel proceeded. It was early morning with a calm surface ruffle, and my solo around-the-island trip was nearly complete, with perhaps a treasure in the making.

It was playtime for several loons, as they water danced and sped by each other with no destination in mind, which enabled my viewing supreme. The one or two that were nearby were a delight, and they seemed to whirl and laugh in my presence, not fearing a foreign encroachment. The close-up markings were identical to those of a newly hatched loon I viewed some two months ago on an adjacent lake, also being red-eyed but deeply suspicious. Being this close was rare indeed for me, enabling my very first such creature close and comfortable.

The loon's markings in white are as permanent as are their annual returns to these chosen lakes and waterways. Perhaps my twenty-minute foray with the lakes' loons was a reminder of the past. Loons assure us of permanence, survival, and fair play. Their many years of migration to this lake carries an example of brotherhood, and it was truly a joy to be amongst them in their peaceful ways.

Soon they assembled and casually advanced up lake, offering a parting perk or two with a familiar and soft tremolo that might have said *see you soon again*. This eastern portion of the lake held its share of man's oldest creature of great worth, and I felt momentarily accepted into their fold as they performed before me their mysterious water fun in play. History says they will return, bringing magic moments for us to enjoy and from which we can learn. (2011)

Loon Wing Act
Pierce Pond Trip

Alas, a single loon resided ahead, and I decided it was to be my only such loon photographic opportunity this day. I noticed early on that he had displayed the familiar wingspread act that is always enjoyable to witness, so I followed him closely with my camera in a high zoom setting. It did come to me that I could fill out my summer's take on a favorite loon activity not often witnessed.(2011)

The Seasons Follow

With the wonders of the winter
now fading,
how softly the land speaks,
and how reassuring the colors all seem.
Happiness begins with the land,
and with the land come hope and goals,
that they will be with us forever,
to provide nourishment and faith for all,
as we move on and grow with the ripples of life
and the shallows of earth,
and the little things of nature.
The passing on of snow and its aging shades
tell us of seasons to come,
as we venture to brighter days of beauty
soon to be upon us
to enjoy.

Snowshoe Pathways
In The March Of Time

It was a gorgeous Saturday, and not only was the midday sun strong, but with it came a cold and frigid delight. Clouds were in and out, and when I came upon the best scene of the trail, the best blue sky prevailed. My six times winter trudging of the new Mingo Loop snowshoe pathway made this my winter favorite, for it offered a solid hour of tree trunks and snowy branches intermingled with tracks and markings of wildlife that remained unseen. Heavy winds moved dry snow to smothering over the packings of earlier hikers, enabling my off trail sinking into softness, which was challenging and better. I did fall and only with difficulty righted myself.

Where the trail crossed a field that bordered the golf course, small trail markers were necessary. Then, disappearing into thick woods, the trail wound around and between but was always distinct with the trampling of travelers days earlier. Numerous snow-laden branches reached down from above to empty their snow load upon me, providing interplay with the trespassers.

Something kept drawing me back on these excursions, most likely it being the satisfying distance alone and the small inclines that challenged on the far half. I sought and found again the one open evergreen setting of huge and healthy trees, embellished at that moment with background blue sky and two gray birches framing the emergence from the woods. Perhaps I only wanted to escape, to explore once again the many wonders of mountain life in these parts, to return and write and enhance this heart's nudgings. Most likely I also choose to bring pleasure to folks of this land and those to follow. It's part of giving back, a dictate these days in the march of time. (2011)

Wildlife Encounter at Hunter Cove

It was mid-April and in the cove there appeared a narrow channel of water making an interesting pattern in the melting process. An ample cloud pattern in the east prevented the early rays from turning the cove to beauty, leaving only a hope for something unusual to happen.

Some three days earlier I had a good sun on a visit to Hunter Cove, although then the midday shine was too bright. Now, a Saturday morning, again there were easterly thin sun-blocking clouds, and only a wandering *something* on the cove ice allowed a chance for redemption. Upon first arriving I had seen that *something* walk across the channel far up stream, an unidentified creature that I never guessed would soon reappear at my end of the cove and turn this trip around.

In the course of time the same animal broke out from the woods slightly up the shore across from me and proceeded to stroll down the cove and closer while along the ice edge. It was here that his abbreviated tail, long legs and medium size identified him as a young bobcat. Soon he mounted the bridge embankment and thereby gained the roadway and bridge I had entered earlier. Then, detecting my presence nearby, he embarked back on ice, but fortunately now on my side of the channel and sufficiently close to be barely discernable as a fine specimen with a dark spotted coat and fluffy white on his chest and hindquarters. Presently, he stopped for several moments to further investigate my presence, and, being satisfied, he casually continued along to my left with no urgency or alarm in his gait. Clearly, his distinctive stubby tail feature identified him as a member of the lynx family and a young bobcat.

In my twenty years roaming these lakes and mountains, a bobcat encounter occurred only once, and this under not nearly as splendid circumstances. Most folks will remark that they have never seen one, although the adaptation to man is evident as just witnessed. This scene will join my prideful collection of a great blue heron in full flight, two newborn young moose being nursed by mother, and a startled shoreline young deer. Indeed, I like to think that living right with persistence and joy brings rewards and sharing. (2011)

Winter Clings Its Best
Edelheid Rd.

After years of exploring local mountains and streams in all seasons, I know secret places of charm and majesty that inspire in special ways. Winter was providing this time. On a snow-drenched day in mid-January, after a snow that fell during a windless night and calm morning, I came upon a quiet stream in full dress of white and wonderment. The snow hummocks decorate a small stream of moving water, while surrounded by abundant snow branches, all being bathed in the soft light of a hazy sun during this mid-morning of country charm.

Snow is nature's way to draw attention to our lives. He who sees beauty in a new fallen snow can cling to all goodness in life. Taken before the breezes came or the sun shone, nature was momentarily beckoning its righteous ways for us to enjoy and be enriched.

Catching a Blue Heron in Flight
Dodge Pond

I had learned from previous visits that a blue heron would be hard to find, but I knew one hung in early morning on the rocks that were now free of water. Indeed he was nearby. I had pulled up to the small parking space just beyond the bridge at the bottom of Dodge Pond hill. I had decided on a new strategy to outsmart this great bird. I carefully moved toward a small pathway that leads to the water's edge but did not enter the path. I could see there was no such bird on the run of rocks where he usually perched. I decided to walk the few steps further, for perhaps he would be sitting on the pond outlet dam and I could catch him before he realized my presence. Indeed, there he was, immediately noticing me and taking to flight. The camera was previously raised and ready, set on high speed and pre-focused where he would pass, but, because of his rapid movement, I had only a split second to shoot. Just before he passed from the opening, I took his picture, wings in full span and he in graceful flight. His body was clear and fully visible as he continued on and disappeared behind the shoreline down lake. It seemed I had outwitted him and soon found a good shot of recognizable wing feathers. In years ahead I have viewed many pictures filmed with exquisite flight and much detail, but this one gave me satisfaction of being my first by clever design. The milestone made me proud and hopeful.

Such encounters at Dodge Pond became a training ground and lit the spark to move to bigger and better birds and their wings of flight. Within two months a friend and I had traveled by motor canoe within the waters of Lake Umbagog National Wildlife Refuge, there to complete the task of bringing home an image of the mighty great blue heron, this time in full flight (see elsewhere in this volume) as he circled our presence and provided the best in opportunity and pride. (2007)

An Overlook of Beauty
Medway Pond

I was into my lunch in for less than a minute when I heard a chirp as two Canada jays flew into branches a little over a few feet away, to which I tossed bits of bread from my sandwich to the snow on my sunlight side. In a flash one bird swooped down and was gone before I could ready my camera for action. Surprised I was to find anything alive and active in this remote and heavenly spot as I relished the moments after my hour-long trek into Medway Pond and its setting.

I was told of steepness of the trail beyond Rock Pond, and so I was thereby being challenged and driven to go. Perfect choice and cold it was as I sat on my jacket for lunch and soon acquired a chill. I had intended to seek out a ledge overlooking Medway, but realized it was satisfying enough to climb just behind the shoreline growth and lean against a dead tree trunk and nourish myself. The setting put me in the sun and I was deeply satisfied.

It is a blessing to possess the desire to explore. The first time in to Medway, where the jays highlighted, is now a week old. Then I passed up the signs to the Medway Overlook, but it registered that I could not resist the challenge to return. It was seven days later, and of partially sunny skies and warm with the Overlook difficulty unknown and irresistible, a sort of "nothing ventured, nothing gained" conundrum. The climb to the Medway overlook was neither too steep nor too deep in snow, only slow and untrampled by earlier hikers. Upon arriving at the Overlook, a climbing task of twenty minutes, Canada jays immediately found me engrossed by the view and the birds soon departed, now a regret. The pond was partially obstructed by intervening tall white pines still snow- laden. As I made for comfort I realized a certain truth with the effort, to bask in this spot.

Many features rewarded: the impressive horizon on a partially sunny day, the characteristic pointed pines indicative of northern growth, the occasional golden beams of sunlight and infrequent glimpses of blue sky, the pond perimeter being gouged out thousands of years ago, the recognition of last week's lunch spot, the feeling of conquering a height in order to view the snowy edge of land and frozen water below, the likelihood that I was the first to arrive this winter. All these were intermixed with gratitude and humility as I studied what lay before me: the quiet feeling and the world before me so calm. The huge boulders, called glacial erratics, seen on ascending, were dropped by the glacial ice pack a mile deep upon the spot where I then sat. These behemoths of old came to leave their mark on the landscape and go unnoticed.

It may be that I have found a home, an escape to the high ground, into a quietness that is reassuring. But I know better. I am reminded that there is much beauty seen from down under as well: sunsets of various designs, melting streams with rock covered snow mounds, a charming lake scene drenched in blue with magnificent white puffs, a full moon reflection just before dawning of the morn, a loon in profile as if speaking in comfort to a close observer, his sounding call of peace, tall trees that rock in the wind and speak to hikers that pass among their roots. Sometimes it is the ordinary we notice and true beauty goes astray along with time. We could take a moment in life to climb on high in order to recall the beauty below. It is happening to me as I speak. The land has its useful heights from which to gaze, as well as enclosures and enclaves below. There is no need to climb to see a rare sunset that serves to bring togetherness and peace. May we nourish on it.

And just now I wish for a great horned owl to cross my path and add his howls to the drone of an aggressive woodpecker that is indeed truly in the woods behind, the two bringing my solitude to a new and lofty crescendo. My heart is charmed and the moments remain. (2012)

Mooselookmeguntic Lake From On High
Words on Love of Land

I had not been on high at **Mooselookmeguntic** Lake. Only rarely had I stood engulfed by the view enclosed. Mostly in years past I resided at water level, and there I had a close relation with the shore and surface. It was there that I camped frequently over several years, and it was there that I came unto special feelings about nature and this land. It was from such feelings that a sort of love affair arose, which was documented and placed within a formal volume that details these sentiments. During those years I witnessed sunsets often and enjoyed the solitude that kept me away from commotion, and I only occasionally wondered about the view on high, that being to where I cast a glance vaguely somewhere up there, while heating chunky soup and enjoying being at water level where all the good things happen at this lake.

Proximity with the water was best. Particularly I recall one evening I crouched against a large bolder in a small cove at water's edge. There I found I was positioned nicely to follow the low and setting sun, at that moment dropping reflections alongside a small island and soon behind. The land came alive as I watched the day's end unfold, and I wondered what was to come next in my life. I was pleased that that picture was pleasure to a retiring preacher and nature lover. Often I came to follow the full moon's upward movement and new reflections, all the while the sun was setting and providing long shadows and twilight. As the evening's reflections came across to me with greater and greater empathy, I thought of the pathways in my life and the glory and grandeur that composed the years. The land and the years were the best, no matter the struggle or the encounters life offered. It was

here at this spot, under the beauty and natural settings, that all came together, that peace prevailed and grew, and it was here that something within me took over, a moment of renewal and restitution. I was carried softly along as I provided for myself under a watchful eye in the sky. Those days are now gone, and I find I still wonder about the days ahead. Yes, my memories will remain, and I may return for one last chance to become one with the land I love.

Some small semblance of savoring of those days did come. We were headed south on Route 17, so we stopped for whatever picture there was of this view from on high. It was grandeur for sure, being Maine's seventh-largest body of water, reaching all the way to the horizon and with surface swirls and islands. On this day the lake before us was a calming blue, one that seemed to be quiet and in waiting. It would have been not too significant a sight, except I found some tall grass blades nearby, and so used them to give less monotony and a closeness reference. Forty long stems, topped with crafty kernels, made my day and became not an oddity in such a scene as this. As I gazed past the blade tops, I vaguely came to rest upon my old familiar shoreline, a place where I once settled in, and I thought again of a familiar cove and small island, a place that brought me forgiveness and true enrichment. The moment was good enough, except I cannot forget and will always recall the low sun's rays of hope on calm water, and a slowly commanding moon providing lightness and warmth for that one evening and beyond.

The picture you hold is familiar to many, except here it is being embellished by nature with weeds and my own reflections from days of old. Enjoy if you can my looking-back moments of precious times in my life. (2009)

Epilogue

Comments from the author seem irresistible. Clearly, my favorites are the following: a splendid cover picture, the fact of three loon sightings, the *Snow Everywhere* originality and the accompanying scene, the imaginative thoughts of *A Child's World*, and the appeal on opposing pages of two life and nature essays, *We Live In A Land*. I tell of what is whole and righteous with nature and its world. Yes, I was in my own glory dealing with my numerous loon findings of last year. And yes, some will even place first the selection of a child's imagination as a worthy and hilarious deviation from the good and gracious norm found throughout.

At this time I am just back from an aborted snowshoe hike to Medway Overlook, undertaken in the melting and warmth of an early spring, as I made a return to safety, thus assuring the finalization of this manuscript. These are my days of looking back more than forward, of a desire to leave a treasure as a personal best, a chance to encourage discernment rather than be an encumbrance. The drive provides first for me and then for my fellowman, all with a beautiful landscape through which to roam. I am often reminded that my followers are more numerous than I realize, so let me offer words of gratitude. Through the sharing with you of the medium of photography and adjoining lines of interpretation, and surely for the many admirers that the effort has discovered, I am truly pleased and ever thankful.

Indeed, knowing that I have entered your lives in a manner of your own kindheartedness and consent brings forth an added treasure to my days.

And, also, may you enjoy these adventures as much as I have.

About the Author

George and his wife, Shirley, retired to Maine many years ago from Massachusetts and Delaware. George remembers his first camera at age sixteen, and he has possessed one ever since. He loves nature and mountains and lakes. His scientific schooling and experience have enabled him to self-publish two prior photo books. Rangeley's beauty drives him as he strives to achieve a keeper on each worthy excursion. George found a satisfying retirement in photography, and in later years his accompanying essays to his pictures became an added creativity and appeal. His many years of picture taking of youth activities at the local Heritage Trust program of EcoVenture have brought that program to greater fulfillment. Today, he seeks an exquisite image of a loon with young chicks prowling a small pond in Rangeley's quiet waters. George and his wife live with two cats in a Cape home central to Maine's best of beauty and comfort.

9